AROUND
BRADFORD–ON–AVON

IMAGES OF ENGLAND

AROUND
BRADFORD-ON-AVON

PAUL DE'ATH

The
History
Press

Frontispiece: Hang Dog Alley (W) *c.* 1905. This picture represents old Bradford perfectly and is just what the visitors love to come and see. The tragedy is that in the 1950s these old seventeenth-century houses were seen as nothing more than decrepit slums and as a result, pulled down. All that remains in the alley today is the single storey building on the left. The small timber structure near the tall chimney is, I believe, a Victorian photographic studio of the 1860s, which survives to this day.

First published in 2003 by Tempus Publishing

Reprinted in 2010 by
The History Press
The Mill, Brimscombe Port,
Stroud, Gloucestershire, GL5 2QG

Reprinted 2010, 2011

British Library Cataloguing in Publication Data.
A catalogue record for this book is available from the British Library.

ISBN 978 07524 3013 3

Typesetting and origination by
Tempus Publishing.
Printed and bound in Great Britain by
Marston Book Services Limited, Oxford.

Contents

Acknowledgements

I would like to thank my parents for once again solving questions relating to some of the pictures. Many thanks must also go to Neil Mattingly for his extensive assistance during the course of this publication and to his invaluable website: www.freshford.com. I am also grateful to Chris Penny and Pam Slocombe for fielding numerous questions relating to various buildings in Bradford-on-Avon, and to Philip and Anthony Wooster for various postcard-related matters. The contributions made by the numerous people I met on my many visits to the locality were greatly appreciated. This book would be most incomplete if it wasn't for the extensive help from all the staff at the Wiltshire and Swindon Record Office, the Bath and Trowbridge Reference Libraries and the Wiltshire Buildings Records. Last, but not least, this publication would never have even seen the light of day had it not been for Derek Mumford, who after much persuasion, agreed to the use of his extensive collection of postcards and photographs.

Town Bridge, *c.* 1925. This was the fine panorama of the town from the Georgian Lodge. The copper-guilt weather-vane of a fish known as the 'Bradford Gudgeon' can clearly be seen on top of the blindhouse. By this time the Lamb Inn had been replaced by a new factory building. The tall Spencer's Brewery to the left of the chimney has gone and the single-storey building with the double-pitched roof behind the LMS goods lorry went in the 1930s.

Introduction

Bradford-on-Avon is a town that remains firmly embedded in my memory from childhood. Although they are only very faint memories, the one that remains is of travelling in my dad's Humber Super Snipe car, crossing the Town Bridge, turning into and heading up Market Street, turning around the sharp corner at the top and climbing up Mason's Lane, which I think was marked up as a 1 in 10 hill at the time. The lane with its tall, soot-blackened walls must have been quite unforgettable for many people over the years. I remember nothing more until passing the Fox and Hounds at Farleigh Wick, where there used to be a solitary dead tree beside the road, which at night always appeared very sinister with its leafless branches stretching out over the road.

For many years now I have passed through the town each weekday going to and from work in Trowbridge, with little time to stop and have a good look around, but I have always considered it a place of great interest that needed investigating, and this book was the opportunity to do just that. Throughout the years since my first memories, the town centre has changed very little, although as usual, the building of housing estates on the fringes have made it a much larger place than when I was a child.

Without any doubt, having travelled through it regularly by motorcycle and now having walked around the town, the biggest headache for the future is one of the absurd amount of traffic that passes through each day. For locals and visitors alike, Bradford-on-Avon is surely becoming ever more blighted by this and a solution is fast required. Needless to say the peak hours are the worst, but it easy to see the effect that school days have too. Long gone are the days when the shops in the narrow stretch of Market Street near the Swan Hotel were able to trade. The building of the Batheaston bypass has a lot to answer for, as the traffic flowing on the A363 through the town virtually doubled soon after its opening. As with many other roads, they have continued to increase at an alarming rate ever since.

In a few of the captions to the pictures, I have referred to missing teeth. The town centre has always seemed quite unusual in that certain key buildings which are no longer standing, for one reason or another, have never been replaced. The first of these must surely be the Priory, of which just one wall remains, but not to be forgotten is the grassy area across the road, where fireplaces can be seen in the wall of the last cottage in Market Street, marking the loss of the end building towards the close of the 1800s. Unfortunately, the wall in Mason's Lane no longer curves around the inside of the corner as it was set back for traffic visibility.

The next location has to be where Knee's store once stood on the corner of Silver Street. Yet another calamity in the name of highway improvements, it has left an odd space, with many reminders appearing on adjoining buildings that there were once houses situated here for a great many years. From this point you only have to cross the Town Bridge to discover the biggest gaping hole of them all which is next to the old Queens Head public house in St Margaret's Street. Two other locations of significance are where the old houses on the corner of the railway station entrance once stood and finally, the corner of St Margaret's Hill.

I have opened the book by visiting the outer parts of the town before delving into the centre. Unfortunately, old postcards of some the former areas are extremely hard to find, such as the Woolley Street district for instance. For some unknown reason, good quality postcards of any part of Bradford-on-Avon are much harder to find than for many of the other towns in the area. Exceptions are postcards of the Tithe Barn, Saxon Church and Town Bridge, which turn up all too frequently.

As in my Bath books, I have also covered the outlying villages, including, a little further afield, Farleigh Hungerford. Some of these places have most probably not previously appeared in print before. One exception to this is Limpley Stoke, which has a third outing in a Tempus publication!

I will close with some notes relating the more significant publishers of pictures in this book. The letters in brackets following the title refer to the relevant publisher below.

A George Dafnis appears in the Bath Post Office Directory as a lodging housekeeper at, 8 Pulteney Street in 1874. Moving in 1900 to 40 Pulteney Street, he is last recorded in 1917. Yet it is most likely to be his son, George Love Dafnis (D), who was the photographer responsible for the views shown here. They seem to have been taken largely during two periods, the first from around 1908 to 1915 and the second during the 1930s. He lived at 32 Sydney Buildings from 1911 until his death in 1968.

Richard Wilkinson (W) was born in Walworth, Surrey, in 1835. Both he and his wife Louisa moved to 33 Church Street, Trowbridge, in 1870. In 1902, Stanley Wilkinson took over the running of the business, but traded as R. Wilkinson & Co. In 1908, it moved to 57 Fore Street, followed by yet another move to 63a Fore Street in 1925. The business ceased to exist in 1939.

Phoebus (P) of Bradford-on-Avon and Widnes account for quite a number of the postcards featured here, many of which have faded badly over the years. As a result, some of these may not appear at their best. As for the business itself, it is a bit of a mystery as there are no entries in any street directory. The company appears to have been run by a Mr Andrews, whose name appears on cards of a similar style to those of Phoebus, but his name is not listed either. Sadly, I also have no information about the connection with Widnes. The number of postcards produced over an approximate ten-year period must have been quite substantial, but despite this, they are very hard to find. Any further information would be most welcome.

There are also a few postcards by Garratt of Bristol (GA). He was a prolific photographer who travelled around much of the West Country over many years and produced hundreds of Bristol postcards and around fifty of Bath. Many of these are extremely hard to find, but his series of the Limpley Stoke area seems to be almost non-existent. I have found only eight in a series of at least thirty in the last twenty or so years!

I have also indicated photographs by Mowbray-Green of Bath (M), who in the course of his 1904 publication *Eighteenth-Century Architecture of Bath*, took a great many photographs, with a handful from the Bradford-on-Avon area. Many of these have never been seen before as they have only recently been printed from the original glass plates and never actually featured in his publication.

I hope that you enjoy the book.

Paul De'Ath,
Bath, 2003

one

Around
Bradford-on-Avon

General View (P), *c.*1905. This view was taken from the canal towpath between the tithe barn and the swing bridge, with the central feature being the fourteenth-century Barton Bridge. The boathouse to its left was later to be completely rebuilt. The track in the foreground leads to the sewage works via the swing bridge and is now tarmacadamed. Today a large number of trees have grown up between the bridge and railway line, leaving only the buildings higher up the hillside visible.

General View (P), *c.*1905. You are now looking from the canal bank to the east side of the Tithe Barn. Sadly, all the farm buildings belonging to Barton Farm have gone, to be replaced by a visitors' car park and bungalow. The goods shed is very notable by its absence, as too is the Trinity National School, which was demolished in 1984. The terraces of Tory, Middle Rank and Newtown are all clearly visible, along with the Zion Baptist Chapel of 1823, which was swept away in the 1960s.

General View, c.1909. Looking from St Margaret's Hill, this picture was taken near to where the lock-up garages are today. The New Mills, later to become part of Kingston Mills, dominate the scene and although they are still with us, the chimney is not. Just below this, is the roof of the old swimming baths, whilst to the left the Town Bridge and the Lamb Inn. On the far left the Town Hall and bank can clearly be seen. Many new houses have since obliterated the tree-lined skyline seen here.

General View, 1948. A more recent picture than many in this book is this view, which I believe was taken from across the River Avon. The vicarage entrance is on the left, with Holy Trinity Church beyond. The two trees in the churchyard have been felled since. On the right. now hidden by a large tree, is the saxon church, whilst in the centre, above the roofs of the cottages is the Trinity National School. Dominating the skyline is Tory, which is seen again later in this chapter.

Church Street, 1908. The central house on the right is Orpin's House and dates from the late 1600s. Beside it is the Trinity Church National School, now called East House. The small building beside it has gone. Facing us is Chantry House and although added to over the years, parts remain from the original 1540s structure. The churchyard railings were taken away for the war effort and the trees on the right have gone, as too has the tall chimney on the weaver's cottage behind them.

Huntingdon Street (P), *c.* 1910. A great deal of change has occurred here. A small housing estate called Huntingdon Rise was built in the early 1960s destroying the wall and gateway on the left. At about the same, across the road, the wall and Samuel Viner's grocery shop also disappeared, to be replaced by a terrace of four houses. The end cottage near the lady in the road was a bakery and was removed soon after the Second World War. Some years later, a road called Church Acre was built there.

Tory, 1935. These must rate as the finest of the houses in this thoroughfare, being good enough for Lady Bowes–Lyon to own one for a while. They date to around 1800 and the only real changes now are the loss of vegetation and the rebuilding of the small rockeries. Many of the other houses to the right of this picture are of a more artisan nature and were in a desperate condition until their renovation in the early 1960s. Demolition was a close call for many of them.

Tory, c. 1909. This is looking in the opposite direction to the previous view. They are also thought to date from around 1800 and command spectacular views across the town. The first on the right is called Mountain Cottage, which has sadly lost the fire mark seen here, followed by Tory House and Pye House. One concession to modern times is that the path has been asphalted. In the background, the chapel of St Mary the Virgin can be seen.

Newtown (P), *c.* 1905. The footpath known as Well Path on the left leads to Tory and an old water fountain called Lady's Well is located in the nearest arch. Sadly, it appears to no longer function. Of the late seventeenth-century houses on the right, only the very nearest and furthest survive. The level of the doorstep of the latter building is now way below road level. The creeper on the wall marks the site of one house which was removed in the mid 1800s. The other two had gone by 1922.

Newtown, *c.* 1909. These are predominantly eighteenth-century houses, although a few are earlier in date. Most are still here to this day. The extension to the Mason's Arms can be seen in the distance. Behind the wall on the right was a strip of land known as Rope Walk, which was no doubt used for rope making. The wall has now gone and retirement homes were built here with the same name. Part of Trinity Church School is also visible, but this and the street lamp are similarly long gone.

Now closed The Mason's Arms, Newtown, c. 1910. This inn was once a pair of late seventeenth- or early eighteenth-century houses, although the single storey addition must be Victorian. It is listed as a public house from 1808 and was bought by the Oakhill Brewery in 1902. The single biggest loss must be the railings. The door where the people are standing has since been blocked up. Note the cannon on the roof and the unusual square chimney pot. The lovely old gabled house next door was gone by 1924.

Right: The Archway, Woolley (P), *c.* 1905. This was once the entrance to Woolley House. Built by 1773, the house was taken down in the mid-Victorian times and never replaced. All that is left is the old coach house and boundary wall. This Gothic entrance dates from the early 1800s. Some of the stonework is in need of repair; the cross on the top and the upper section of the right pinnacle are both missing. The ivy has gone and a five-bar gate replaces the stylish ones seen here.

Below: Woolley Terrace, *c.* 1905. Just off of Woolley Street is Woolley Terrace, a row of nineteen cottages constructed around 1830. This is number 7 which has been renumbered as 13 and has gained the name of 'Bien Venue'. The houses appear not to have altered very much, although a couple are in a state of extreme dereliction. The lady is probably Mrs Chapman. The greenery around the doorway has gone and the windows have been replaced in an unsympathetic leaded style.

Trowbridge Road (Y), 1910. This tranquil scene is hard to imagine these days, with all the traffic that uses it now. Looking from the end of St Margaret's Street, Junction Road is on the right and a relatively recent track leading to St Margaret's Villas is on the left. The fine early nineteenth-century villas on the left represent the best of the property along this road. Amazingly, their iron railings are still with us. Sadly, many overhead cables spoil this scene today.

Trowbridge Road (P), c. 1905. The Plough Inn was once part of Regent Place. Built in around 1830 as two houses, it opened as a public house c. 1855. Now just called the Plough, the front garden has been adapted for car parking use. The entrance to Regent Place is on the right and is wider these days. Across the road, the open space where the railings stand has been filled with new housing. Telegraph poles, street lights and a new pedestrian crossing have altered this view greatly.

Trowbridge Road (W), *c.* 1910. Looking towards the town centre, the end of Westfield Villas is just visible on the left. This is followed by a long row of houses known as Beaconsfield Terrace, which was completed by 1899. The removal of their railings during the war has left the boundary walls in a mess. The hanging sign for the Plough Inn can just be seen again in the distance. Unimaginative modern street lighting has replaced the decorative variety seen here.

The Canal Tavern, Frome Road, *c.* 1910. Originally a mid-Victorian house, John Adey became its first licensee around 1907 and remained so until 1913. It now has extensions to the rear, but is still a Wadworth's house. The building appears to be painted white and marks from a pitched roof can be seen on the wall. The window shutters no longer exist. An extra window has been added to the right of the door and a large bay window to the left. Today, one feature totally out of place is the reconstituted stone porch.

Barton Bridge (R), 1909. Very little has changed here as far as the river crossing is concerned, but Barton Bridge, a scheduled ancient monument, is not the main feature. The small bridge in the foreground takes prominence instead. However, this and the iron railings are of early Victorian construction. The large trees are no more, as a brick pillbox was constructed here during the Second World War. Much of the wall on the right is missing and the remains require restoration.

The Swing Bridge, Bradford-on-Avon.

The Swing Bridge (D), *c.* 1905. This rustic feature used to lie on the Kennet and Avon Canal, approximately half a mile from the Tithe Barn in the direction of Avoncliff. A track crosses here which leads to the sewage works owned by Wessex Water, but the current structure would not make for a good postcard view as it is a modern steel bridge, with a timber footbridge alongside for pedestrians to cross the canal. The swing bridge is usually left in an open position.

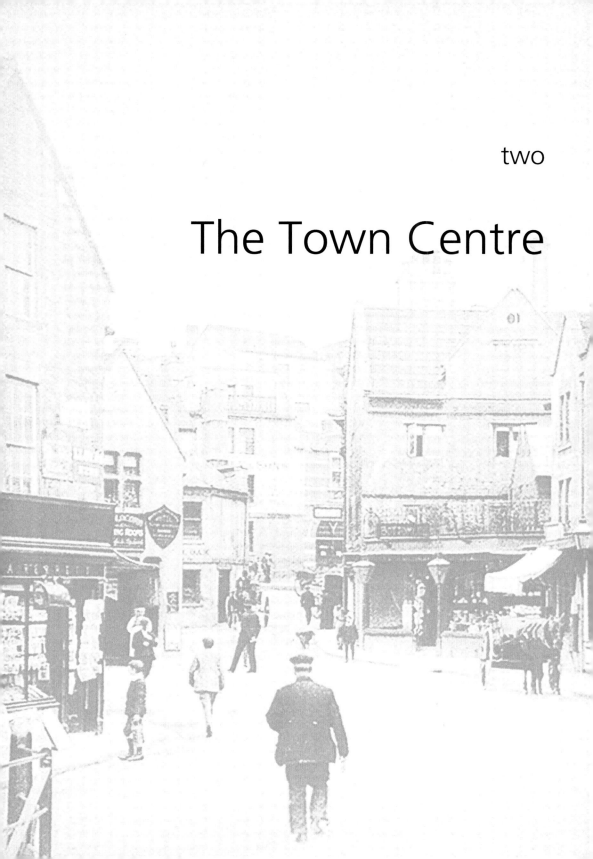

two

The Town Centre

St Margaret's Street, *c.* 1909. On the right is the entrance to Morgan's Hill Independent Chapel, now the United Church. To the left is the saddler's shop owned by William Bolwell. Both this and the adjoining houses were pulled down in 1963. On the corner of St Margaret's Hill with the large enamel sign was the bakery run by Henry Burgess. These days, it is the premises of the local Christian Fellowship. The tall chimney on the house next to the horse has now been severely truncated.

St Margaret's Street (W), *c.* 1930. How different this view is today, with a roundabout and traffic everywhere. Unfortunately, the three old gabled houses, most probably of seventeenth-century origin, which included Kate Bricker's sweet shop, succumbed to the demolition men in March 1935. Long before this though, in the eighteenth century, they were home to the Old French Horn public house. Note the petrol pumps outside Central Garage and the enamel sign advertising Knee's of Trowbridge.

The Green Tree Tea Shop (W), 1934. Also in St Margaret's Street is number 11, a fine house that was built in the eighteenth-century. Its days as a tea shop are long over as it is currently the premises of Green Tea Health. It was run by Margaret Wood for just one year, before being taken over by Miss Bryant. The stonework has been restored and the railings have been replaced, but not in a Georgian style. Also, the tree and flowerboxes have since been removed.

The Swimming Baths (R), c. 1910. These baths were constructed in commemoration of Queen Victoria's Diamond Jubilee and large financial contributions were made by John Moulton and Lord Fitzmaurice. New baths were built in 1971 near St Margaret's Hall, but they were demolished and replaced by the new library and museum which opened in 1990. Sadly, the three-storey house in Bridge Street had been pulled down some time before 1966 and the one in the distance was to go a few years later.

The Blindhouse, 1887. Next to the inquisitive men is the Blindhouse, dating from the mid-eighteenth-century. It is thought that there may have been an earlier building here. It has been called a chapel, but this seems unlikely. Nevertheless, it was used as a toll-house for beasts going to Saturday market, as well as an ammunition store for the 1st Wiltshire Rifle Volunteers. Conservation work has allowed the iron straps to be removed, as well as the opening-up of the little window.

The Blindhouse, c. 1910. This is a view from the riverbank next to the New Mills. In 1826, a riot occurred in the town over the increased price of potatoes and although the ringleader was caught and placed here, the mob extracted him by tearing off the roof! Of particular note is the Queen's Head Inn partially visible throught the trees. It closed c. 1912, but as far back as 1732 it had been a public house. Believed to date from the seventeenth century, it was sold when Spencer's Brewery closed down and the adjoining three-storey house which they also owned was demolished and never replaced. The façade was rebuilt soon after and the property reopened as tea rooms in 1926.

Town Bridge (Y), 1910. Despite the poor quality, this is a great picture. The bridge has nine arches and was originally a packhorse bridge. Two late Norman arches survive from the thirteenth-century, which are ribbed and pointed and can be seen in the previous picture. The bridge was widened in 1769 by rebuilding the western side. To the right side are the New Mills, which later became a part of Kingston Mills. Note the paved road crossing and the tall chimney, both now long gone.

Town Bridge, c. 1912. This is one of the rare Bath Tramways Series postcards, showing the part of the bridge that was widened in 1769. The ford is on the left and was still used in the 1800s for some horse-drawn vehicles, but is not there anymore. There have been other changes, such as the loss of the large trees, not to mention the Lamb Inn and other nearby buildings. The large sign advertises 'Spencer's celebrated old mild, bitter beers and double stout, wines and spirits'.

The Bull Pit, *c.* 1930. Named after the once-popular sport, here is a view that has changed little over the years. Looking from the end of the Town Bridge, the mill building on the riverside replaced some earlier two–storey buildings in the 1890s. Avonside Construction Limited on the right has since become home to C.S. Bowyer Limited, funeral directors. One feature to note of the Bull Pit today is that the road has been raised up by about a foot, presumably as a flood defence measure.

Hang Dog Alley, *c.* 1908. Looking along the passage, the entrance into Church Street can clearly be seen. Of the large gabled house on the right, only the angled part where the two buildings come together survives. This was once a coffee tavern. Even the narrow window has now been removed, with large panes of glass replacing those seen here. This was once one of the most picturesque parts of the town. With the severe traffic problems in the town, this is a very useful thoroughfare.

Silver Street, *c.* 1905. Here is a better opportunity to see those buildings that have gone forever. The fine frontage of the Lamb Inn is on the right. Next door is Willson's chemist shop with a large pestle and mortar above the door, which went in 1961, whilst the single-storey shop was removed in the 1970s. Across the road was the White Hart Temperance Hotel, which was pulled down in 1967. Note the enamel signs on the newsagents shop and the urinals near the Swan Hotel entrance.

R. Seymour, Silver Street (W), 1905. This is Robert Seymour's shop at 10 Silver Street, where he traded from around 1904. In 1921 he moved into the tiny shop next door, where he stayed until 1949. Animals were slaughtered at the rear of the premises and was until recently a butcher's shop, but is now a restaurant called Little Venice. The second-floor frontage has been rebuilt in a similar style, but the use of ashlar blocks, instead of rubble stone, betrays the buildings real age.

H. Brunt, Silver Street, *c.* 1923. Something of a contrast to the previous picture is this view of the same shop taken some twenty years later. By now it was run by Herbert Brunt, who was here from 1923. Two years later he went into business with a Mr Lanham. This is more likely to be the normal amount of meat displayed, as opposed to that seen in the previous picture. The shop frontage is not too dissimilar, although the large window has been split into four vertical panes, with the stonework painted red and white.

Silver Street, 1900. On the left was a clothier's house from about 1700, which became the Angel Inn in the 1730s. Renamed the New Bear Hotel by 1809, it is now converted into flats and called Silver Street House. Alongside is T. & E. Taylor's wine shop, now the Bunch of Grapes public house, whilst opposite is another part of their wine and spirit business. A large board on Sundial House advertises 'Rogers AK Pale Ales'. Next to the alley known as 'The Cut' is E. Hunt's drapery shop.

The King's Arms Hotel, Coppice Hill 1902. The King's Arms was built soon after 1790, replacing the White Hart, and is seen here in August 1902. Still open, but no longer a hotel, its appearance is much plainer, as the large sign, the painted advertising and the leaded windows have all gone. The two gables on the adjoining seventeenth-century part of the premises have also been removed. After the closure of Ruddle's Brewery, it became an Usher's hostelry, but is currently owned by Greene King.

Coppice Hill, 1939. This is a view looking up from the Shambles. No doubt life in these seventeenth-century cottages is a lot more pleasant now than it was in olden times. The scene is very similar to this day, excepting that the single-storey building on the left has gone, as too have the three distinctive brick chimneys. Further up the hill is a house with a large doorway which was the forge. The entrance has since been replaced by stonework and a window, all in keeping with the surroundings.

The Shambles (R), *c.* 1910. The doorway on the left is an original feature of this fifteenth-century lock-up. The Royal Oak Inn was trading as early as 1798, but with Robert Clark as landlord it closed in 1912. In the adjoining late-medieval houses were Ellen Cabell, confectioner, and Fred Archard, tobacconist and hairdresser. The half-timbered façades are most likely from the 1600s. The Georgian building on the right was Arthur Wheeler's outfitters shop, but was replaced in 1932 by a new post office building.

Right: The Shambles (D), *c.* 1935. Here is a similar view, but by this time Mrs Cabell's premises had become a tea and coffee shop and a modern shop front had replaced the older one. The new post office extension can clearly be seen. The eighteenth-century shop front on the far right is now part of the Halifax Estate Agents. Next door, with the display of produce, are the premises of Albert Davis & Sons. He began trading in Market Street in around 1903 as a fishmonger and opened here in 1929.

Below: T.W. Coupland, The Shambles, *c.* 1917. This is number 4 in the Shambles and looks very similar today, but has now been painted white. Thomas Coupland ran this shop, selling groceries and patent medicines from around 1895. Standing in the doorway of the Victorian shop front is Ernest Coupland. In 1923 Walter Coupland took over the business, until A. Davis & Sons moved in six years later. Needless to say, the enamel sign advertising baking powder has gone.

The Shambles, *c.* 1903. Here we can see the old houses from the opposite direction. They are thought to have been built some time between 1350 and 1450. A pillared market hall stood at the end below Coppice Hill, but collapsed in 1826. A shopping area here since the Saxon times, Payne's is now a jewellers called Jewel. At the end on the left is part of the King's Arms Hotel, whilst in the distance is William Norris's chemist shop in Silver Street.

The Shambles *c.* 1955. These shops on the left were rebuilt in the 1930s and are now occupied by Ex Libris and the Dorothy House. The post office building is opposite. The two Tudor-fronted shops remain unspoilt, although the furthest has lost its stone-tiled roof and old Royal Oak Inn has gained shop windows. As Tillion's China Shop today, it has large plate-glass windows. The pennant sandstone slabs seen here in the centre of path have since been replaced with concrete slabs.

Above: The Post Office, 1907. In 1901 the post office replaced a shop which probably dated back to the 1600s. It moved here from further up Market Street and it looks as clean here as it does today after a recent restoration. This included painting the timbers on the end of the building cream instead of the more traditional black. Once more, the Georgian house next door can be seen before its untimely removal, and on the right is the Swan Hotel with a large window advertising Spencer's Brewery.

Right: Market Street 1906. This narrow road once known as Horse Street has been ruined by the incessant flow of traffic. On the left is Albert Scrine's Colonial Meat Co. with its splendid hanging lantern. Further up and encroaching into the road is Albert Mayell's china and greengrocery business. Now it has closed, the windows are painted black. The White Hart Temperance Hotel is on the right, whilst next door are the premises of Ann Smith, tobacconist. Note the canopy over the door – sadly, long gone.

The Swan Hotel, Church Street (P), *c.* 1905. This is the principal hostelry of the town, as it has been for a great many years. The present building dates from the eighteenth-century and today the frontage is painted black and white, with a picture of a swan painted in the circular feature. The decorative hanging lamp has long been removed, as too have the flower boxes. The window to the left of the door has been altered to match the others. In the distance is Walter Willson's chemist shop.

Market Street, *c.* 1925. Here, the Swan Hotel appears much as it does today. You can see the newly installed ground floor windows which replaced those seen above. The fountain and lamp were provided in 1919, in memory of those lost in the Great War, but they were removed shortly after the Second World War. The shop to the left of the Swan Hotel has now gone as it was turned into a garage for the post office.

Church Street, 1909. The Old Bank House on the right is a private house now, but in the 1700s it was a public house called The Red Lyon. In the 1820s it became a printer's and then a bank in 1878. The Georgian façade masks two buildings. The nearest part is seventeenth-century, whilst the furthest is fifteenth-century. Across the road in Market Street is Albert Nichol's grocery store. He was also an agent for Gilbey's wines and spirits. Today, this is The Dandy Lion public house.

H. Stokes, Church Street, 1909. Part of this shop at 3 Church Street can be seen above. Henry Stokes stands in the doorway, he was here from about 1905 until 1916. At this time, it was the Bradford Dairy; the name can seen printed on the fabulous globular gas lamp. Sadly, this has now gone as has the panelling below the windows. More loss of decoration includes the fanlight, which was replaced by a plain sheet of glass. Bishop, Longbottom & Bagnall, solicitors occupy the premises today.

Above: The Town Hall, 1914. Built in 1854 by Thomas Fuller of Bath, the Town Hall put an end to the seventeenth-century New Market Tavern. Next door, in 1871, the North Wilts Bank replaced shops of a similar age. Used as Council offices until 1910, it then became a cinema until 1920, and following recent renovation, it is St Thomas More Catholic Church today. Sadly, some of the decorative stonework above the top floor windows is missing, as too are the decorative lamps beside the main entrance.

Left: C. & M. Boorman, Market Street, *c.* 1903. Now belonging to the Stroud & Swindon Building Society, this shop was a drapers owned by Misses C. and M. Boorman. It appears to be an eighteenth-century building and whilst the shop front remains much the same, the rest of the frontage has been rebuilt, resulting in the loss of the projecting façade on the middle storey. The building on the right, belonging to the London Central Meat Company, was rebuilt in around 1930.

Bedford & Horton, Market Street, 1890. These shops date from the 1700s, with the one on the left belonging to Anna Bedford and Mary Horton. In around 1880 they opened a Berlin Wool depot, but within five years changed to confectioners. The two ladies stayed here until around 1900. Andrew Dando now runs an antique shop from here. Both of the large vents have been blocked up. On the right is John Selby's boot and shoe warehouse, which is the Dandy Lion public house these days.

Market Street, c. 1925. The fine mid-Georgian house on the left is currently the home of Avon Antiques, whilst alongside is the fish bar of W. & O. Manners, which was previously a post office. Beside this is the Conservative Club, now renamed the Bradford-on-Avon Club. For some reason, the raised part of the parapet is missing today. The seventeenth-century gabled building next door is now occupied by Best Laid Plans, gifts and stationary shop. Pippet Buildings (on the right) narrowly escaped demolition in the 1970s.

Market Street, *c.* 1920. This is a very picturesque part of the town and was once known as Pippet Street. Safety has dictated that iron railings must now run along the top of the wall. The shop behind remains unaltered, but is no longer used, and the decorative street lamp is no more. The house occupied by Jeremy Jenkins is on the right and next to it is a fine seventeenth-century twin-gabled house. The house over the alleyway has since lost its stone tiles and gained a large window.

Market Street, 1907. Even at this time, the shop on the right was out of use and so too was the shop in the adjacent gabled house. They both date from the seventeenth-century. The adjoining Georgian buildings were occupied at this time by Frank Summers, a blacksmith, and Albert Davis, a fishmonger, whilst Silby & Keen, bootmakers, occupied the lighter-coloured building beyond. Apart from the loss of some of the chimneys, not too much has changed here over the years.

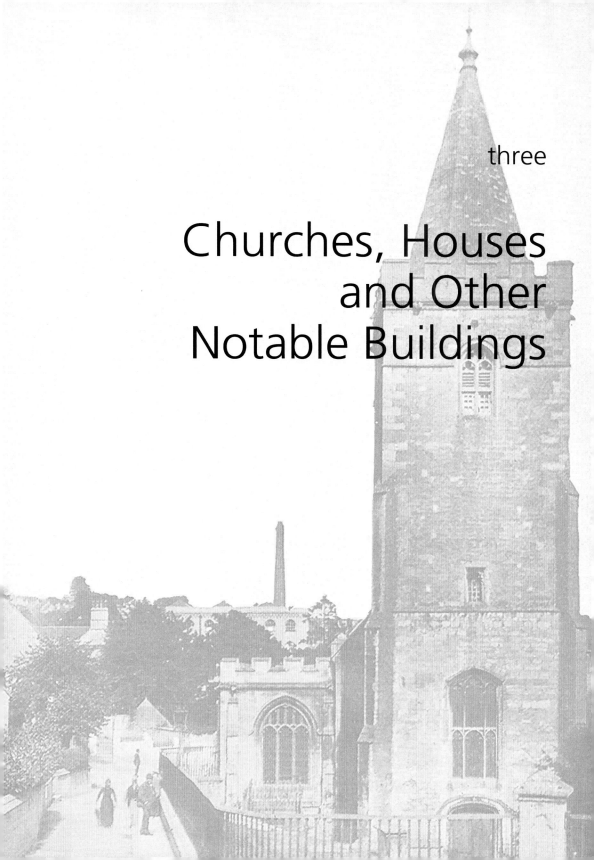

three

Churches, Houses and Other Notable Buildings

Saxon Church (M), *c.* 1900. This picture of the church of St Laurence is looking from the back garden of a cottage in Church Street. The earliest known reference to the church was by William of Malmesbury in the 1120s, who believed it to date back to the eighth-century, but it may well have been built for the nuns of Shaftesbury in the eleventh-century. In 1614, Gifford Yerbury described it as a 'chappell' and in 1712 the rector John Rogers set up a free school for boys here. In around 1856, during repairs, two stone angels were discovered above the chancel arch, but as it was still a school with a separate cottage attached, restoration could not commence until the site had been acquired in 1874. This side of the building was relatively untouched by later additions. There were chimneys which were removed during restoration.

Opposite below: Parish and Saxon churches (R), *c.* 1910. The Saxon church can be seen here in context with its surroundings when viewed from the gardens of Abbey House. On the left is the parish church of Holy Trinity, which is believed to date as far back as around 1150, but could be earlier. Canon Jones was appointed vicar in 1851 and found the building in a terrible state, so restoration was carried out between 1864 and 1866. Little has changed, although the crosses on the eaves have since broken off.

Right: Saxon Church (Y), 1910. This is a view from the corner of Church Street. By this time the cottage had been removed, leaving these ugly sloping buttresses to support the church. These, and the scar left by the roof, make one think it would have been best left alone. J.T. Irvine, the architect in charge of the restoration, resigned over the trustees' decision in 1881 to demolish the cottage for this very reason. These buttresses were eventually reduced in size in 1933. By the time this picture was taken, two of the windows had been unblocked to let in some daylight and these now contain leaded-glass. Below this, it is quite apparent that a lot of new stonework was put into this end wall, which was rebuilt in the 1700s. Both the railings and the lamp-post are no more.

PARISH CH; &

SAXON CHURCH.
BRADFORD ON AVON.
R. 1125

Holy Trinity Church, 1887. Here is the other end of Holy Trinity Church showing the fifteenth-century tower in all its glory. In the background are the Abbey Mills, built by Richard Gane in 1875. The tall chimney was removed in 1971 and the mills were finally closed by the Avon Rubber Company in August 1995. At the end of the road, where the people are standing, the new wall, built in front of the Saxon Church following the removal of adjacent buildings, can be seen.

Holy Trinity Church (Y), 1910. Although a very similar picture, I thought it would still be worthwhile including it as the angle of view is a little different. By this time, a flagpole had been erected on top of the tower. The railings around the church were taken down for the war effort and this also meant that the streetlight mounted on top of the railings had to go too.

Right: Christ Church (P), *c.* 1905. Christ Church is relatively recent as far as churches go. It was designed by G.P. Manners of Bath and was built by the Jones Brothers of Bradford. Construction began on 12 September 1839 and was completed within two years. Many improvements were made in 1875 to what, at the time, was a very plain church. This view is looking from the top of Mason's Lane. The three large trees in the foreground are no more, but otherwise it still looks virtually the same.

Left: Christ Church. Although this undated photograph of the steeplejacks was poorly taken, I felt that it had to be included. These brave souls standing at the top of the spire were pictured from Mount Pleasant. A cross was located on top of the spire, which can just be seen in the previous picture. Here, it has been removed and this is presumably the reason why the workmen were working there at the time. This process was repeated in 1981, but with a permanent ladder fixed to the spire.

St Mary the Virigin, Tory, *c.* 1904. Thought to date from the fourteenth-century, this chapel or hermitage was mentioned during John Leland's visit to the town in 1540. The chapel is on the left and has a small cottage adjoining it. A document of 1587, however, refers to it as St Leonard's chapel. At the time of reconstruction in 1869, only part of the eastern wall survived. Since then, the location has altered little, apart from the loss of the tree. A fantastic view of the town can be had from here.

The Vicarage, 1914. A short walk along the riverside will present this view of the vicarage. Known as Kingston Place, John Leland recorded a building here during his visit to Bradford. Although mostly demolished in 1842, the present building dates from 1846 and still contains some of the original features. It was the home of the Reverend Jones from 1851 to 1885. These days, a conservatory has been added to the left side and a large bay window replaces the nearest ground floor window.

Wesleyan Chapel, *c.* 1910. At the top of Coppice Hill was the Wesleyan Chapel which was built in 1818, with the schoolhouse on the right. March 1959 saw the last service as the congregation had dwindled in number. Gradually, it fell into decay and lost its roof, but was rescued in 1982, becoming an open-air swimming pool. Today, it is a tragic sight as even much of the walls have crumbled. The impressive façade remains intact, apart from the windows. This grand building surely deserves better.

Above: Hall's Almshouses (M), *c.* 1900. The almshouses were established in 1700 by John Hall and they provided accommodation for four old men and their wives. A sum of £40 per year was left for the upkeep of the properties, with any remainder split between the occupants. In 1890 they were restored by Horatio Moulton. Note the wonderful old houses on the left which, at a later date, lost their gabled ends. The council thought fit to compulsory purchase and demolish these late seventeenth-century houses in 1963. By comparison, the almshouses have changed little, with only the greenery removed from the frontage. The setting is not so pretty now, as a traffic island is sited in the middle of the busy road. Also, large direction signs and an electrical cabinet have been placed where the barrow is parked.

Opposite above: The Cemetery Lodge, *c.* 1913. A search was made in 1855 to find a site for a new burial ground. Work started here in September of that year and was completed the following July. The lodge house stands at the entrance to the cemetery on the Holt Road and was built for the use of the sexton. It is not too dissimilar to this day, although the tall chimney on the left side of the house is missing and the gateway has been walled up. The flower beds are noticeably lacking these days.

Opposite below: Technical School, *c.* 1904. Construction of this school started in October 1895, with J.B. Silcock of Bath acting as architect. Later renamed the Fitzmaurice Grammar School, it closed in 1980 and stood empty for a time before becoming part of a sheltered housing scheme. Looking from Lorne Villa in Junction Road, today all the leaded windows have gone and those by the entrance have been elongated. Also, the front garden has been lowered, leaving a terrace along the building's frontage.

Bradford-on-Avon.
Technical School.

Christ Church School, *c.* 1905. This National School was opened in 1847 at Mount Pleasant, with Captain Septimus Palairet of Woolley Grange paying for the construction of the buildings. The school has since moved to new buildings nearby. One very noticeable feature from this angle today is the lack of greenery in the background. The wall in the foreground has several breaks in it and the ornate stone gateway has gone. The school buildings have lost the pinnacles on the eaves.

Westbury House, *c.*1913. Originally named Bethel House, it was standing by 1720. In 1791 the house was the scene of a riot and from 1911 to 1974 was used as offices for Bradford Urban District Council, but has now been converted to flats. The central chimney on the house has gone and the gardens are now a public open space, with the war memorial standing in place of the stone urn seen here. The wall on left has had the railings removed, the gate piers have been recently restored.

Druce's Hill House (M), *c*. 1900. Seen from the corner of Abbey House is the grand Druce's Hill House. It was built in the 1730s for Anthony Druce, but he went bankrupt in 1740. The Bailward family moved here towards the end of the century and remained here for many years. During the Second World War, the premises were used as a troop canteen. The most noticeable difference today is the loss of all the railings. The windows have been restored to match those of the house on the left.

Below: Kingston House (D), *c.* 1935. A grand example of Jacobean architecture, Kingston House is thought to have been built in around 1580 by John Hall, a clothier. Later known as the Hall, it became the residence of Earls and Dukes of Kingston. In 1773 the property was bought by the Manvers family, but by the early 1800s it had fallen into decay and was used as a wool store. Stephen Moulton J.P. bought the house in 1848 and set upon its restoration, during which the south front was almost entirely renewed.

Belcombe Court (M) *c.* 1900. A grade one listed building, Belcombe Court is situated along Belcombe Road. The origins of this house lie in the sixteenth-century. The property was owned by the Yerbury family for nearly two centuries, following John Yerbury's purchase of land in 1722. He built a clothier's house here, along with a factory and named it Bellcombe Brook House. In 1734 his son Francis employed the services of John Wood the elder, who added two large wings, one of which is seen here. The east wing, featuring the clock, is thought to date back to the late seventeenth-century, whilst the circular turret is from the following century. It was used as dovecot, but may also have been a prison cell. A riot nearly occurred here in 1787 when 1500 weavers marched from Trowbridge, but they returned peacefully, possibly after seeing two small cannons set up by John Yerbury in the windows.

Opposite above: Old Church House (M) *c.* 1900. This fine building dates from the early sixteenth-century and is located in Church Street. Between 1874 and 1903 it was the Free Grammar School, but today it is used as the Masonic Lodge and Holy Trinity Church Hall. The house has been altered a lot as it lost its central gable and dormer windows following restoration in 1925. All the large ground floor windows were rebuilt to the same design as the central ones on the upper storey. The group of windows nearest on this level have been removed and those next to them have been moved to the left. The very large window in the end gable is now quite different and the coping stones are no longer featured. The tree at the end of the house has gone, along with the railings and gate. One considerable loss today is that of the lovely twin-gabled house on the end. This used to be the Ship Inn until 1850 and was demolished in 1922, leaving just a paved area where this house once stood.

The Priory, 1914. This magnificent old house dates from about 1460 and was built for Thomas Rogers, who was a sergeant at arms. Numerous additions were made over the years, especially in Georgian times. It was not really a priory and was known as the Methwins for many years, named after the Methuen family. In 1848 the Sisters of the Holy Trinity took over ownership and this is where the name of the Priory came from. Having remained unoccupied for some years, in 1937 the estate was broken up and sold for redevelopment, resulting in its near total demolition the following year. All that remains is the end wall, standing only as high as the second storey. This is the fantastic view that would have greeted you as you rounded the corner at the bottom of Mason's Lane showing the main entrance to the house. The wall on the left was set back as a road improvement. This tragedy shows just how little respect was held for historic buildings in the past.

Old Cottage, 1914. This was the gardener's cottage, which once belonged to the Priory. It is believed to have been built in about 1830 and is a single-storey building. The house has also been called the Witch's Cottage. At last, here is a scene that has barely changed to this day. The only major differences are the placing of a window in the centre of the thatched roof and the line of decoration along the bottom of the thatch is no longer there.

Frankleigh House (P), *c.* 1905. The house originates from around 1630, but was extended and restored in 1848, when the south and east fronts were rebuilt. The property was a spa for a while in the 1700s and was occupied by Dr Daniel Jones. The house was advertised in 1879 as a Grammar School called Kingswell Court. In 1917 it became a private house again, but returned to being a school in 1935. Today it is Frankleigh House School and a large wing has been added to the left side.

Northleigh (P), *c.* 1910. The house appears to have been constructed in about 1870. Its first resident was a Mrs Hopkins, followed by George Lopes D.L, J.P. The last resident was a Miss Kennard and from 1931 the house was vacant. After the Second World War it was turned into flats, but by 1956 was empty again. This time it was not so lucky and the house was sadly pulled down. Within a couple of years an estate of bungalows were built and fill every last space of the former property.

Berryfield House (P), *c.* 1905. The earliest reference to this house is in 1830, when it was described as Burfield House and occupied by a Mrs Timbrell. This appears to be a misspelling of Bearfield House, which was its name for many years, but by later Victorian times it had become known as Berryfield House. It was home to Ezekiel Edmunds J.P. and Michael Palmer J.P. during much of this time. By 1939 it had long been empty and on 30 August 1939, Wiltshire County Council requisitioned it for use as a maternity hospital and is now awaiting a new use following recent closure. In these modern times, a much smaller pair of front doors have replaced the originals and the window canopies have gone. Also, the beautiful conservatory has been removed and a large covered area built in its place. Sadly, a grotesque tall flue has been attached to this side of the house. The building behind is now three storeys high, but despite the changes the house maintains its grand appearance.

Kingsfield House, 1907. Located just off of Whitehill, this house has a prominent position overlooking the town and was built in the early 1860s. It was renamed Martins in 1929 after the family. The man with his dog is most likely Mr Martin himself. A fine stone porch has been added as well as a large 1970s extension to the left side, which is indistinguishable from the original building. The fence and gate have gone as the field in the foreground is now part of the gardens.

Woodleigh House, 1924. This large house sits between Woolley Street and Holt Road. Dating from about 1836 and called Sevenfields, its first resident was the Reverend Henry Harvey. In around 1850 it was renamed Woodleigh House and in 1933 it became Conigre House. After the Second World War the house was used as a hostel, but by the late 1950s it was turned into flats and now stands in the middle of a housing estate. The chimney stacks have now gone, as too have the large fir trees and creeper.

Woolley Grange (P), c. 1905. The house dates back to around 1610, when it was owned by the Baskerville family. Known as Woolley House, Captain Septimus Palairet carried out much work on it and from 1846, he changed the name to Woolley Grange. In 1990 the house opened as a hotel and still appears very similar to the way it was in this picture. The chimney stacks remain although the pots have gone and there is still some greenery on the house, but not as much as seen here.

Barton Farm, *c.* 1940. This is a gem of a grade one listed building with some parts dating from the late Middle Ages as well as the early eighteenth-century. It was a grange of Shaftesbury Abbey and as the farm was in existence before the end of the first millennium, an even earlier house most likely stood here. In the sixteenth-century it was described as being the manor house of Bradford. The farmhouse and fields were leased from Sir Charles Hobhouse in the late 1800s to Joseph Chard. His son Ernest ran the farm until 1971, when it was purchased by Wiltshire County Council for a country park. Two years later Ernest retired and the Wiltshire Historic Building Trust took over the farmhouse. The vegetation has been removed from the house and the railings remain, but not the timber fence.

Tithe Barn (Y), 1910. The tithe barn was constructed in the early fourteenth-century and for many years was in the hands of the Hobhouse family. They handed it over to the Wiltshire Archaeological Society in 1914, who undertook urgent repairs. In 1939 the barn was passed to the Ministry of Public Buildings and Works. They carried out a major restoration over a ten-year period and more recently it has come under the guardianship of English Heritage. Sadly the working farmyard days are long over.

Tithe Barn, *c.* 1930. Here is the interior of this vast building before restoration. By this time, it was no longer used for farming, but stored old carts instead. Today the building is totally empty, which is a real shame. Long, metal, tie-bars cross the roof to hold the building together. During restoration, the roof was removed and every timber inspected. The north-west wall was completely rebuilt, then the roof was re-lathed and the stone tiles were replaced.

Above: Kingston Mills (W), *c.* 1906. These rubber mills founded by Stephen Moulton stand on the west bank of the River Avon and were built in 1806. In 1848 he bought the mills and Kingston House, as well as some other abandoned mills and set to restoring them. Waterproof clothing was a mainstay for the new company, but gradually other rubber items were produced here over the years. Sadly, the main mill buildings were replaced in 1973 with modern factory units.

Left: Kingston Mills, *c.* 1900. Here is another view of the rubber works. The large brick chimney was replaced in 1913 with an iron one, but this too has been taken down. The two storey brick building remains, albeit derelict since the end of rubber production here in 1992. In the foreground are some items from H. & R. Crisps' Avonside Ironworks in Bridge Street. New houses here have replaced the ironworks and large trees partly obscure this view today.

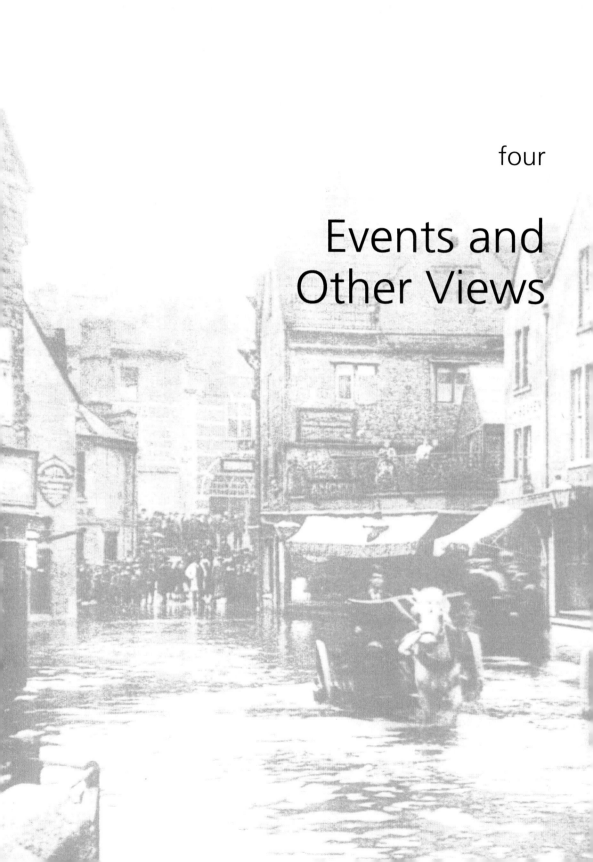

four

Events and Other Views

Flooding, 1903. Flooding of the River Avon has been a familiar event for many over the centuries. This was the state of the river on 16 June 1903. As can be seen the river has exceeded its normal width by a great deal. This is a view downstream from the town centre. The building inundated by the water was a boathouse located next to the almost completely submerged Barton Bridge. In the distance there is a lane leading up to Newtown where several people can be seen watching the event.

Flooding, 1903. This is the same flood as shown above and it was taken on the same day. The town centre was awash, but horses and carts could still get through. This view from the end of the town bridge shows the Lamb Inn on the right with Willson's pharmacy next door. Sadly both of these buildings no longer exist. The Lamb Inn was closed when Usher's Brewery took over Spencer's Brewery in 1914. Two years later it was pulled down. Opposite is the entrance to the Swan Hotel.

Flooding, 1925. Yet another view of serious floods in the town, this time on 3 January 1925, when a charabanc tried to make its way through the deluge. By now the Lamb Inn had been replaced by a rubber tyre factory, but the chemist's shop was still standing. Uncles, the boot makers had been replaced by Ward's Library. The corner of Knee's store can be seen as well as a large painted notice for Usher's Noted Invalid Stout on the front of the King's Arms public house.

Flooding, 1925. Looking in the opposite direction we can see the same charabanc from the previous picture crossing the town bridge. There are actually several people hanging onto the side of the vehicle. It is preceded by a brave horse and cart and followed by a small van. Closer inspection of the picture will show that by this time the house to the right of the Queen's Head Inn had gone.

Flooding, 1933. Here is an excellent photographic postcard showing how seriously the town once flooded. In the background can be seen a throng of people watching the progress of the car through the flood waters. This is a view looking up Market Street (previously Horse Street). Mark Uncles, boot makers shop is seen again on the left, whilst another of the town's 'missing teeth' is the building on the right, H.J. Knee's household furnishing store.

The Start (P), 1905. The title of this card is a little bit misleading, as it could be taken in one of two ways. Is it meant to represent the starting point of the bus service to Bath, or does it show the first day of services between the two towns? Either way, the location is outside the Swan Hotel and the passengers seem ready to depart even though the bus driver does not. The vehicle is one of the Milnes Daimler buses that were purchased by Bath Electric Tramways in 1905.

C. Dainton's Bakery Van, *c.* 1910. This picture shows Frank Dainton standing with one of his father, Charles's horse drawn vans. With a basket of bread on his arm, there is no doubt about his type of trade. Charles began the business at 20 Silver Street in the mid 1880s, but moved to 1 Bridge Street not long after. In 1916 Frank eventually took over the business, by which time it had moved to 25 Bridge Street. He carried on trading there until the late 1920s.

E.D. William's Van, *c.* 1910. Displayed here is a delightful picture of Ernest Williams sitting in his van, which is not too dissimilar to the one seen in the previous picture. Mr Williams was a baker, grocer, bacon curer and provision merchant who had a shop at 11 Silver Street. He opened in about 1910 and traded until after the First World War. His last year working at the shop was in 1921, when he was described as a grocer's manager.

The Co-operative Society Delivery Van, *c.* 1922. This postcard, photographed by H. Foster of Bath, shows the proud driver of one of the Bradford-on-Avon Co-operative Society Limited delivery vans. HR 6322 was made by the All American Truck Company of Chicago and was registered on 8 April 1922. The society was established in 1862 and by the Edwardian Age had a membership of 2,100. It was not possible to have one big store in the town, so there were a number dotted around the centre.

H. Paul Hayman lorry, *c.* 1935. The view shown here was photographed by F. Lindsay of Trowbridge. Presumably one of the men is Harold Paul Hayman with his Bedford W 2 ton lorry. I believe this picture was taken at the end of Holt Road, just after the junction with Woolley Street. Registered on 31 January 1935 as WV 7071, the lorry appears to have seen better days by the time it is shown here.

King Edward VII Funeral Service, 1910. Here is a view from a window looking along Church Street. The service was in held in Holy Trinity Church in May 1910. A lot has altered since this time and not necessarily for the better. All that remains of the mill buildings with broken windows are ground floor façades and all the windows have been filled in. To the left, the rubble stone building with the louvres has gone completely and the next property is now only two storeys high.

Coronation Procession, 1911. The procession through the streets was in celebration of King George V's coronation and took place over two days. Thursday 22 and Friday 23 June saw the decorated streets come alive. This view looking across the bridge shows a small band approaching and many more marching across the bridge. Onlookers were not just confined to the streets as can be seen by the man stood on the far left. The Lamb Inn can be seen immediately behind him.

Carnival Procession, 1910. Both this and the picture of the Coronation Procession were taken from the same location and by the same photographer. This is one of the many annual town carnivals held over the years. The postcard was sent on 6 August 1910 shortly after the event. In the background the Queen's Head public house (now the Three Gables) can be clearly seen along with a three-storey house to its right. This is now one of the towns 'missing teeth'.

Bradford Carnival, *c.* 1910. The date and precise location of this view remains uncertain, but the reason for the picture is not a mystery. These three groups of people were all awarded first prize at the carnival. The display on the right is pretty self explanatory as it represents a model of the old water wheel. The one on the left is a decorated bicycle with a mast and a union jack flying from it. In the centre is a floral display set around a pram.

Bradford Carnival, 1911. The delightful display seen here shows the pupils from the Undenominational School for Girls getting ready to take part in the town carnival. This school was located in Mason's Lane. A considerable number of girls are lined up in order to pull the chariot on its journey around the town, unlike today, where brightly illuminated carnival floats are hauled by tractors instead.

Bradford Carnival, 1912. This bizarre creation was made for the 1912 carnival and appears to have been photographed in fields behind Trowbridge Road. The old bicycle has had a quick makeover on the wheels, which have some kind of wildfowl drawn on the white parts. The costume is something else, although its length seems rather likely to have become caught up in the rear wheel.

Carnival Procession, *c.* 1920. Times have moved on since the previous carnival pictures. This would appear to have been taken in the 1920s. The float in the foreground is decorated with various flags including the star spangled banner. The car on the left was registered AM 7832 and is a 14hp Scripps Booth that was first registered on 18 July 1917, whilst on the right can be seen Uncles & Son, boot makers shop at 2 Silver Street.

Bradford and District Motorcycle Club, 1912. An impressive line up of veteran motorcycles outside the Swan Hotel was gathered for a meeting of the local motorcycle club on 12 April 1912. A world apart from motorcycling of today, it is surprising to see the number of sidecars carrying their rider's partners and even a child. Through the window an advertisement for the locally brewed Spencer's beers can be seen.

Recruiting Day, 1914. This building, for me, is the equivalent of the Empire Hotel in Bath. It is totally out of character with its surroundings, but has enough character to be allowed to remain. The Town Hall was put up for sale in 1910 and remained so for the next four years. This picture was taken on 20 August 1914, when around 1,000 people turned up for a recruitment meeting for the First World War, hence the reason for the largely male turnout.

Red Cross Hospital Barge, *c.* 1917. During the latter part of the First World War a barge, named The Bittern, was used by the Red Cross Hospital Volunteer Aid detachment to transport soldiers from the town to the Red Cross Hospital. This was established in the Old Court at Avoncliff. The barge was also used to collect the soldiers from Bath, a three hour journey. The horse used to pull the barge can clearly be seen on the left, whilst the steersman is standing at the rear of the boat.

Red Cross Staff, *c.* 1917. Here is a group photograph that was taken at the Technical School, later to become Fitzmaurice Grammar School. As well as the nurses, there are local dignitaries and other Red Cross staff seated behind a number of stretchers. The first convalescent soldiers arrived at Avoncliff on 22 July 1917, where the staff had to look after between 80 and 100 soldiers.

Red Cross Hospital Fête, 1917. This picture may well have been taken at Avoncliff as the event was in aid of the Red Cross Hospital, but it shows a group of the children who attended the fete that day. No doubt this was one of many events held to raise funds for the running of the hospital.

Unveiling of the War Memorial, 1922. A very solemn event was the dedication of the Town's War Memorial which took place at 3 o'clock on 2 August 1922. The ceremony was undertaken by Viscount Long of Wraxall, the Lord Lieutenant of Wiltshire and was attended by many dignitaries and locals. The memorial is located in the park near Westbury House and stands in memory of the 126 towns people who died during the First World War.

Bradford Cricket Club, 1907. The photograph was taken outside the front door of Barton Farm. The town had several cricket teams and these were the Bradford-on-Avon second team. Whilst the main team was in the West Wilts League, it appears that these men would play against other local teams that were not in any particular league.

Bradford Football Club, 1908. This is a group photograph of the Bradford–on–Avon Church Lads Brigade football team. Despite the smartly initialled shirts and caps that they are wearing, the rest of the outfit was left to the individual as can be seen from the variety of socks and shorts worn. They seem not to have been in any league, but just played against other minor local teams. One match in the middle of January 1909 was against the Trowbridge Fire Brigade, who beat them 3-0.

Bradford Football Club, 1909. The 1909-10 team of the Bradford–on–Avon Association Football Club, who were in the Wiltshire League are seen here. The club was founded in 1883, when their ground was located near the old gas works. In 1906 a new ground was opened, which is where this picture was taken. By the end of the 1930s the club had ceased to exist and the ground became part of Fitzmaurice Grammar School. They were winners of the Wiltshire League Championship in 1907.

Bradford Football Club, 1912-3. Here is the Bradford United Football Club at the end of the 1912-13 season, when they were in Division 1 of the Bath League. The cup that is displayed was won as a result of winning the Trowbridge Junior Cup. After a successful semi-final, where they beat Leigh Institute 3-0, they went on to play Shaw and Whitley in the final on 26 April 1913. This finished as a goalless draw, so three days later they had a replay at Trowbridge, when they won 2-0.

Bradford Leigh Sunday School, *c.* 1920. This is a most delightful picture of the Sunday school children and their parents from Bradford Leigh. Sunday school meetings were no doubt held in the Wesleyan Methodist Chapel which is situated along the lane towards Holt. Although no longer used as such, the chapel still stands and is a small green painted corrugated iron building, which looks more like a large shed than a place of worship.

Foreign Mission Festival, 1907. This event was held on Wednesday 21 August 1907 and was organised by local Wesleyans and Sunday schools. They wore clothing that represented a number of eastern Asian countries, with the Bradford-on-Avon contingent dressing as Ceylonese. After parading through the town, the group ended up at Leigh House. Various placards were made such as those seen here advertising the Colombo Industrial School and the Batticaloa Medical Mission in Ceylon.

Annual Liberal Club Dinner, 1910. The gathering took place on 12 March 1910, not long after the Liberal victory in the general elections, with Mr John Fuller M.P. in charge of the proceedings. Held in the local swimming baths due to the large number of people attending, there must have been upwards of 150 people packed into this room. For the catering staff, getting the food to the tables must have been a feat in itself as the room is so cramped.

Brass Band, *c.* 1910. The band was assembled in the grounds of Priory Park and may well have been Spencer Moulton's Town Band. The band was formed just before the turn of the century as a result of an amalgamation with the Bradford-on-Avon Amateur Brass Band. Ever popular at the numerous carnivals and fetes in the town, the band was led by a Mr Busby.

Rowing at Barton Bridge, *c.* 1910. Another form of sport that was and still is popular in the town is rowing. This is the 'Maiden Four' of the Bradford Rowing Club seen heading away from the landing stage of the boathouse. The boathouse is still situated here and has expanded in size over the years. They seem to be receiving a lot of attention from the spectators on the bridge. The town centre is beyond the bridge, with Barton Farm just off to the right hand side of the picture.

Cottage garden, 1908. This battered postcard dating from 29 August 1908 shows Mr Fox standing in his front garden, having won first prize for his floral display. The house was at 131 Trowbridge Road, but was renumbered to 30 and is located on the right hand side as you leave town. Unfortunately, these houses have lost their railings. This particular house has also lost its small balcony above the bay window, but still retains the coloured-glass front door.

Farmer at Barton Farm, c. 1913. The man is dressed in a traditional West Country smock and is seen standing outside the porch of Barton Farm. The ornate gate is still in place to this day. The sender of the card has written to say that 'he looks like a maid: but he isn't, he is a useful member of society'. In fact he was most probably the milker at the farm and is holding the large bucket used to collect the milk.

The Railway Station, 1897. The station staff and travellers are frozen in a moment in time as they pose for the photographer at the local station. This must have been during Queen Victoria's Diamond Jubilee celebrations, as at the entrance to the platform there is a foliage arch, topped with the letters VR above the royal coat of arms. There is much to see, from the numerous advertisements to the man with the hand cart. Little has changed here, although electric lighting and a telephone kiosk are inventions that would appear here at a later date.

Troops at the Railway Station, 1903. These are some of the troops from E Company, 1st Wiltshire Rifle Volunteers at the railway station. They had recently received new uniforms and slouch hats. The occasion would most likely be when they travelled to Dorset for joint manoeuvres with the Dorset Volunteers at East Lulworth in August 1903. Having seen these soldiers, I wonder whether the boy sitting on the cart became one himself, or was called up to fight in the First World War?

Railway Station Staff, *c.* 1910. This undated photograph shows the full complement of staff at the local railway station. I am convinced that this postcard view was taken inside the goods shed where the full staff is pictured, from the station master to the porter. With the ending of goods traffic at the station in 1965, the shed was removed and the site has now become a part of the car park.

Bradford-on-Avon Signal Box, *c.* 1920. This is a photograph of the signal box that controlled the goods yard at Bradford-on-Avon. It was located a short distance from the Bath end of the station and in the background, Barton Farm can be seen. With the end of goods facilities it was no longer required and was subsequently demolished. The goods yard is now used as a car park. A clue as to the approximate date is the acetylene lighting on the signalman's bicycle leaning on the steps.

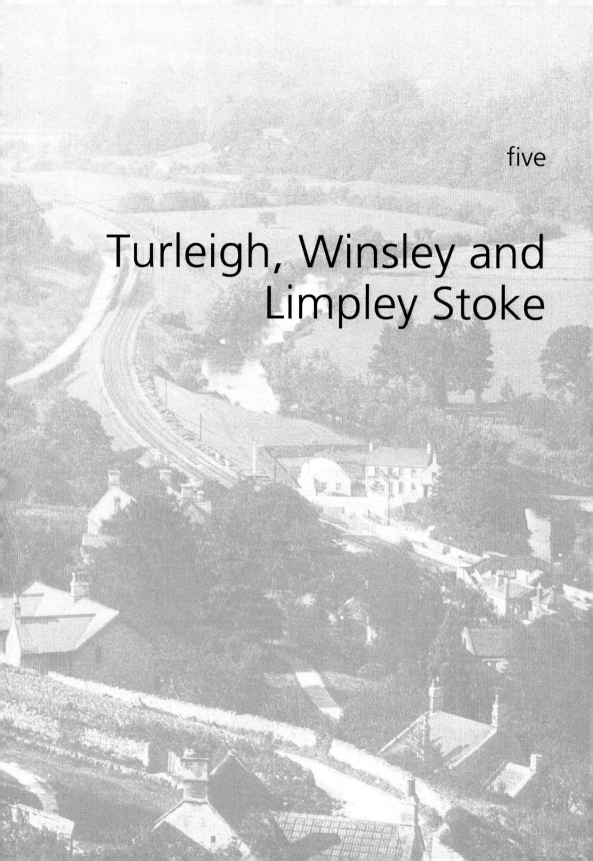

five

Turleigh, Winsley and Limpley Stoke

General View, Turleigh (D), *c.* 1935. This is the view as seen from the lane leading from Bradford-on-Avon to Winsley. The partially ruined wall in the foreground has been replaced by a garage and the lean-to behind it has been replaced by a fine extension to Marsh Mary Cottage. On the far left, the building with many windows is the 1912 extension to Brooklands, whilst on its right, with the ivy, is Turleigh Cottage. The area below this is still very overgrown today.

General View, Turleigh (P), *c.* 1905. Shown is the view as seen from just above the lane mentioned previously. This time Marsh Mary Cottage is on the far left. Both the front door and canopy have now gone. The view has changed very little, although it is now totally obscured by trees. The small ones on the right are now at least fifty feet tall! Just beyond the bend in the lane is the Malthouse. One new cottage has now been built in corner of the field opposite this building.

Turley House, Turleigh (P), 1907. The building is now called Turleigh Manor House and dates from the late seventeenth- to early eighteenth-centuries. This view is not visible from the road, but has altered very little. The single dormer window has been replaced by a pair on this side as well as the front façade and two lines of slender fir trees line the main path. The road through the village can be seen in the background. A message on the postcard explains that it had just come out.

Brooklands, Turleigh (P), 1907. Constructed mostly in the early 1800s around earlier buildings, in the 1920s it was renamed Turleigh Mill, but is now called Turleigh House. The conservatory on the right was replaced in 1912 by the then owner Mr Leverson-Scarth by the two storey extension with the numerous windows seen in the first picture. Much of the ivy has gone as too have the Victorian canopies. An extra window on the upper storey has now filled in the gap.

War Memorial, Winsley (D), *c.* 1930. This view is looking in the direction of Bradford-on-Avon and has not changed too much. The war memorial has been engraved with the dead from the Second World War, to add to the 13 who died in the Great War. The grass island is now surrounded by a triangle of kerbing and the walls on the left have been rebuilt further back in order to accommodate a footway. Today, lots more trees hide the houses along the road.

Opposite: Old Cottage, Turleigh, *c.* 1910. The cottage is located next door to the old post office. The rangework stone façade would suggest that it dates from the Victorian period. The front gardens of both buildings have been removed and this one is now unfortunately a concrete hard standing for car parking. Since this time, the timber porch has gone and the chimney has been rebuilt in reconstituted Bath stone. The climbing tree has also gone, but at least the stone footway remains intact.

Winsley (G), *c.* 1930. Now we are looking in the opposite direction, showing the other side of the War Memorial. To the right can be seen the tower of the parish church, which is now hidden by trees. The buildings on the left belong to Manor Farm. Note the primitive timber striped road sign warning of the school, the end of which can be seen where the main road turns sharp left. The main road turns a sharp left by the two gate posts belonging to the village school.

Schools, Winsley (Y), *c.* 1910. Here is the local primary school as seen in the previous picture. It was built in 1866, enlarged in 1894 and was disused by 1972. The left side is now called School House, whilst the right side has become Winsley Social Club. The entrance gate has been relocated beyond the bicycle. As for the buildings, the turret and many of the decorative ridge tiles have been lost and a row of bushes have grown up behind the boundary wall.

Winsley, *c.* 1920. Here is a view looking towards Bradford-on-Avon with the Seven Stars public house on the right. The beautifully built wall on the right has been taken down to accommodate the car park and the hanging inn sign has also gone. The schools can be seen on the left beyond the trees, which have since been felled. The wall on the left has been rebuilt and a bus shelter now stands above the old well. The old cottages in the centre of the picture have lost their thatched roofs.

Winsley (G), *c.* 1930. This view along the lane next to the school shows some of the small old cottages in the village. The previous picture shows these buildings with thatched roofs, proving that they must have been renewed in the 1920s. The single-storey building survives, but has lost the top part of its chimney. The small window has been enlarged and a large modern doorway replaces the one seen here. The railings have also gone, to be replaced by a wall.

Winsley (D), *c.* 1930. This view has altered very little. The nearest cottage was built by Ambrose Heal in 1818 and remarkably, the decorative railings have escaped destruction. Note the old square stone chimney pots on the end house. Sadly, very few of these remain today and these are no exception. The oldest part of the church of St Nicholas is the tower with the remainder being rebuilt in 1841. The railings around the tomb have gone, as too has the structure on top of the tower.

Old Houses, Winsley (P), *c.* 1913. The location is looking along the lane in the opposite direction from the last picture. These delightful cottages were built in 1617 by the village carpenter but have since lost their thatched roofs and the eave on the right hand cottage has been truncated to just above the upper floor window. All of this has been a disaster for the character of these old properties. The garden wall has since been rebuilt and the trellises around the doors have gone.

Rock House, Winsley, 1907. Rock House with its well-tended garden is situated nearly opposite the Seven Stars and is currently called Scarth. The house originally consisted of three cottages and these formed the main part of the house as seen here. The differing window styles give some indication of this. These were originally thatched and date back to the 1600s. The first written evidence of the house appeared in 1732. The wing to the right was added in 1902.

Winsley (W), c. 1915. These buildings are on the edge of the village, opposite the lane leading to Murhill. The railings have gone, but the wall on the left is just the same. The ivy covered house is now called Wheatsheaf House, but was the Wheatsheaf off-licence for many years. The shop behind the pram was a confectioners at this time, but it later became a grocers. Today there is only a little ivy on the façade and the shop doorway has been blocked up. Next door is Spring Cottage.

Winsley Sanatorium, *c.* 1910. The hospital opened on 16 December 1904 for the treatment of tuberculosis. It was later renamed Winsley Chest Hospital. Following closure in 1985, redevelopment took place for its conversion into retirement homes. As Avon Park Village, the only recognisable part today is the three storey façade nearest the camera. Instead of being at the end of the building as seen here, it is now roughly in the middle. Fountain Place stands where the building on the left used to be.

Winsley Sanatorium, *c.* 1910. Here we have a scene of tranquillity, with croquet being played on the lawn and a gardener tending to the flowers. None of these buildings remain. They were located at right angles to the main hospital block, the rear of which was to the left of the picture. New buildings have been erected here and are known as Deanery Walk.

The Chalets, Winsley Sanatorium (G), *c.* 1930. All of these chalets have disappeared since the closure of the hospital. A recently constructed three storey block of flats called Kingfisher Court stands here instead. The edge of the stone quarry can be clearly seen. These chalets were built on stone backfill, the original quarry floor being many metres below. This picture would have been taken from an upper floor window in the main sanatorium buildings.

Winsley Sanatorium, *c.* 1920. Here is a group of people outside one of the chalets at the hospital. Judging by the dress, I would imagine that this is a group photograph of some of the sanatorium staff. This photographic postcard was produced by W.G. & A. Collins of Bradford-on-Avon who had a studio at 10 St Margaret Street from 1913 until 1923.

The Cleeves, Murhill (D), *c.* 1935. This is a view along the lane looking in the direction of Winsley and is still very heavily wooded today. The lane on the right leads to Murhill House. The only real change is that the long line of railings on the left have been taken down, along with the post and wire fencing on the other side of the road. Note the tall stones to stop overrunning of the verge. These are still standing.

Murhill (G), *c.* 1930. The lane on the right hand side in the previous picture will lead you to this location, although it has been photographed from the lane on the left and in the background, through the trees, is Freshford. Only in wintertime would it possible to see it from here today. The path and many of the large trees have gone as a car parking area has been constructed for the nearby house. Just in case you were not aware, the notice reminds you that 'These woods are private'.

The Canal, Limpley Stoke (G), *c.* 1930. Here is a view looking towards Bath from the canal bridge at the bottom of Winsley Hill. This view is now blocked by trees overhanging the right hand side of the canal. However, all the large trees on the left canal bank have gone, as too have the boat sheds. Following a great deal of restoration, the canal is back to the condition seen here and boats can frequently pass along this section.

The Canal, Limpley Stoke (D), *c.* 1907. This picture was taken towards the end of the straight section of towpath seen in the previous view. Notice how clear the canal banks have been kept. The towpath is still just as wide, but there are no longer any cattle roaming free or cowdung to step in. The woodland on the right has all disappeared and is now just a field.

The Canal, Limpley Stoke (D), c. 1907. This stretch of canal is about 600 yards from the road bridge in the direction of Dundas and is just around the corner shown in the first picture. Note the built out section, where the canal could be blocked off when a length was to be drained. These are called stanks, but this one may originally have had stop gates installed. Since the canal was renovated, the stonework has been repaired but the gates are still missing.

Stokeford Bridge, Limpley Stoke (G), c. 1930. This is a very similar view to that shown in my second Bath book, but was taken more than twenty years later. Today, a long line of trees alongside the riverbank have replaced the logs and obscure the view of the houses. The bridge remains visually very similar to this, despite more recent widening on both sides. The ivy on Bridge Cottage has been replaced by a large rose bush and a new stone canopy has been fitted above the doorway.

Limpley Stoke Railway Station, *c.* 1930. It is no longer possible to stand here anymore, as the station closed on 3 October 1966 and the platform was removed. In fact most of what you can see here has gone, apart from the station building just to the right of the train. This survivor is now well cared for and hopefully, one day, will again serve passengers on this line. A light snowfall can be seen on the roofs of the buildings, with the Hydro visible through the trees.

Westralia House, Limpley Stoke, 1924. This view from across the railway line shows the house facing out across the valley. Located between the village shop and the manor, it is set back from the road and adjoins a property called Monk's Garden. Built in 1738 as Weir House, from 1911 to 1924 it was known as Gloucester House, then Westralia House, returning to Weir House in 1933. The conservatory has since been removed, but apart from an extra dormer window, it remains very similar.

The Manor, Limpley Stoke, *c.* 1920. The manor was originally the Dower House and dates from the seventeenth- and eigtheenth-centuries. After many years in use as a school, it was purchased in 1954 by a civil engineer. The following year building work began which destroyed the whole character of the house. The earlier three-gabled part was pulled down and the rear section, visible to the right, had the pitched roof replaced with a flat one. Words fail me as to how anyone could do such a thing.

Opposite above: The Hydro, Limpley Stoke, *c.* 1907. This is a view looking from Woods Hill and is almost hidden by large trees today. The Hydro was founded in 1860, and a surprising amount of change has occurred since then. It now has an extra storey added to the right wing, with a metal fire escape in the corner. The tall block of chimneys has gone, along with the flagpole and the square feature adjacent. Also, the tower on the right has lost its balustrade. In the foreground is Apple Tree Cottage.

Opposite below: General View, Limpley Stoke (W), *c.* 1900. Here is another view, now mostly obscured by trees, which was taken from the Warminster Road. In order to see this today you need to stand on top of a wall and avoid a tall boarded fence. Many more houses have been built on the hillside since, but the scrubby area near the large tree is still there. On the right is the Hydro, with the railway footbridge and Stokeford Bridge visible. Finally, faintly in the far distance is Dundas Aqueduct.

Penelve, Limpley Stoke, c. 1905. Penelve was completed by 1903 and is seen here from the edge of the valley, with Midford Lane behind. Many alterations have been made, the most dramatic being a two storey extension to the left side, which has resulted in the loss of the two eaves. The lean to on the right side has been replaced by a large conservatory. In 1924 the name was changed to Hilltop by the then owner Mrs Burges.

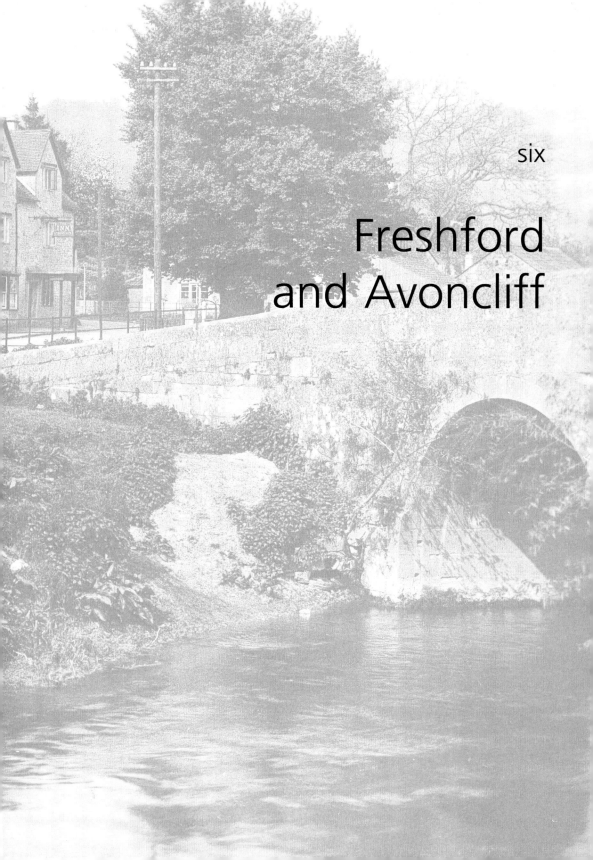

six

Freshford
and Avoncliff

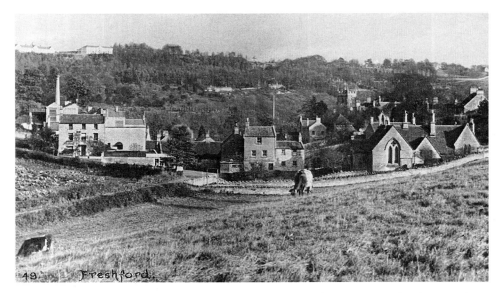

General View, Freshford (P), *c.* 1905. This view was taken from the Tyning. Standing between the trees high on the hill is Winsley Chest Hospital, whilst below it is the brewery chimney and a house named Tyning View. The field on the left of Freshford Lane now has houses built on it. The tall house directly in the centre has become the post office, with the Church Room of 1896 on its left and South Cottage to the right. A new school building now obscures the school on the right.

Park Corner, Freshford (D), *c.*1930. Looking from Ashe's Lane, this view can no longer be seen due to new housing. The upper storey of Beech Cottage (1890s) is on the left and in the centre is Corner House, dating from around 1760. To its right are two much older, smaller cottages, one having lost its proper roof. A shed and Woodpecker house (1895) stand on the site of more cottages. The Primitive Methodist Chapel is visible in the background along with the roofs of Upper Mount Pleasant.

Above: The Rectory, Freshford (P),
c. 1905. When viewed from Church
Hill, this house has a prominent location
on the hill above Avondale and the
old brewery. Situated on the corner of
Crowe Lane it is now named the Old
Rectory after a new one was built in
1979. The house was designed in Bath
by Charles E. Davis and built in 1859.
It appears very much like this today,
although the creeper has been stripped
from the building.

Right: The Tyning, Freshford, *c.* 1930.
By the time this picture was taken the
street lamp had lost its glass top. The
tall houses next to the chapel belong to
Sharpstone Place and were built in the
1840s. The nearest is called Roseneath
with Glenholm adjoining. The two storey
house beyond is known as Woodleigh.
Unseen, but situated between them is a
much older cottage called Middle House,
which has just been restored. By this time,
a second gateway had been made into the
Methodist Chapel.

Wesleyan Chapel, Freshford, *c.* 1905. This narrow lane leads to Sharpstone and the first building encountered is the Methodist Chapel. Built in 1854 on the site of two old cottages, it is now no longer in use. Following closure in 1995, the property was converted into a house, like so many others. At this time, the wall in the foreground was partly removed to allow space for car parking. The gate has also since been moved to where the man is standing outside the front door.

Church Hill, Freshford (P), *c.* 1905. This view from the top of the hill shows Avondale, the brewery owner's house, in the centre. On the right, partially hidden by the wall is the Old Parsonage dating from *c.* 1637. Another ancient house with its stone-tiled roof known as Tudor Cottage can just be seen through the trees on the left. Both this house and the two gateways no longer exist. A new house has been built here in a sympathetic manner.

Right: Greyhound Inn, Freshford *c.* 1910. This inn and brewery was situated in West Street. Ushers took it over from Wilkins Brothers in 1922 and closed it in 1964. Unfortunately the top storey has been removed resulting in the destruction of its unique appearance. The 'Wilkins Bros.' sign is still there and an older blue one for the Freshford Brewery can partially be seen beneath it. Although the lamp has gone a greyhound sign still hangs from the location seen in the picture.

Below: St Peter's Church, Freshford (P), *c.*1905. The tower is the oldest part of the church, dating back at least to the second part of the fifteenth-century. The nave was rebuilt during Georgian times and then the chancel in 1859. The following year the old clock was replaced with the one seen here. Recently restored, it is inscribed 'Hallett, Bradford 1860'. The greenery on the church and the big tree on the right have gone and only one upright grave survives.

Post Office Stores, Freshford, 1907. The bakery and stores were built in the 1830's and run by the Morris family for many years. The post office moved in the 1950s, the bakery shut in 1960 and finally the stores closed in 1989. The bakery was bought by the church in 1991 and converted into a church hall and the stores reopened as Freshford Antiques. The doorway with the stone lion beside the bakers van have been rebuilt as an archway, with the lion moving just across the road.

Left: The Hill, Freshford, *c.* 1907. This view was taken from the top of Church Hill and remains largely unaltered to this day. Sadly the large and prominent street light has gone, as too have the railings belonging to Corner House. This house, which dates from the late 1700s, had a new façade constructed in the early 1800s, with these large distinctive Gothic windows. During the 1830s it became Mr Cliffes Boarding School. The sign by the wall reads 'Danger, Cyclists Touring Club'.

Opposite below: The Hill, Freshford (D), *c.* 1935. Further down the hill is this old house which looks very similar today, apart from the loss of the right-hand chimney. This is the Old Manor House (also known as Freshford Farm) which dates back to the late seventeenth-century. On the left side there is a crest, which for some reason has never been completed, whilst between the upper windows is a Sun Insurance fire mark which is still there, unlike the road sign for the railway station.

Freshford House (The Manor), Freshford (D), *c.* 1935. The house originated in around 1720 and this view of the south side shows the left bay added by Thomas Joyce in about 1800. The right bay was added in the 1880s by Thomas Isaac, along with the large conservatory on the right. In the 1950s the property was almost destroyed by a developer who sold off the outbuildings, stripped the interior and then applied to demolish it. An American couple bought it just in time in 1956.

The Hill, Freshford (D), *c.* 1929. The large house basking in the sunshine is known as the Old House or Porch House. Reputed to have been built in 1623, it was altered in around 1780, which included a new façade. Little more was done until 1910 when much of the interior was renewed, including the attic windows. After the war it was converted into six flats. The railings opposite, belonging to Temple Court were removed for the war effort, whilst further down the hill is Hill House.

The Inn and Bridge, Freshford (D), *c.* 1930. This scene remains very similar today, although speed limit signs now adorn the entrance to the village. The village nameplate is still there with its Somerset Automobile Club initials on it. The bridge across the River Frome was built in 1783 and replaced a much older one. Possibly the greatest loss was the elm tree which had an old semicircular stone seat at its base. The pig shed on the left completes this rural scene.

The Inn, Freshford (D), *c.* 1930. The Inn was known until the early 1920s as the New Inn. The lettering 'A.M. 1713' is carved into the central gable and represents the rebuilding by Anthony Methuen of a much older building, which may have been a hospice belonging to the monastery. In Edwardian times, the roof lost its stone tiles and was raised to bring it over the gable ends, thus totally altering the character of the old building. Sadly, the hanging sign has gone and Ushers Brewery is no more.

River Bridge, Freshford (P), *c.* 1905. The bridge is located next to Freshford Mill in Rosemary Lane. Taken from the road, the mill is to the left of the bridge and the photographer is facing in the direction of Sharpstone. Examination of the picture shows that much of the stone has failed on the bridge piers and has been replaced with engineering bricks. The only real change in recent times has been the unsympathetic replacement of the railings with ones that resemble scaffold poles!

Aqueduct, Avoncliff, *c.* 1920. Here is a view from a track leading from the end of Green Lane in Turleigh. The landscape has altered significantly. The large area of woodland behind the houses has become a field, whilst the opposite has occurred to the slope below the houses on the skyline. A line of trees now obscures the closest end of the aqueduct, but the Cross Guns can now be clearly seen. The real test though is to try and imagine this scene without the canal.

Avoncliff Halt (P), *c.* 1910. The railway station was opened in 1906. It survived the Beeching cuts of the 1960s and still has these two short platforms. Mundane off-the-shelf steel railings have replaced all the timber fencing leading to the platforms. Mesh fencing now runs along the rear of the platforms. The gated crossing has been removed and a small shelter stands where the station nameplate was located. The weir is today hidden by a large mass of trees and vegetation.

Railway Line, Avoncliff, *c.* 1910. The station can no longer be seen from here as trees now obscure the view. The stables on the far left have been converted into a house, but in the process the gentle pitch of the roof has been lost. The pumping station partly obscured by trees has now lost its chimney and has been converted into a house. Mill House to the left of the railway remains, but Avoncliff Mill opposite is now very overgrown and derelict.

Avoncliff Mill and Weir (W), *c.* 1880. Here is a closer view of the mill, with the buildings looking quite different from those in the previous picture. Despite the postcard having been touched up, I believe this was an earlier photograph reproduced much later as a postcard. Despite a new wheel and millstones being installed in 1860, I suspect that this picture was taken shortly before 1883, when part, if not all, of the mill was completely rebuilt.

Avoncliff Mill, 1907. The mill had been here from as early as 1585. In 1718, when it was sold, it was split into two, but the part that was used as a grist mill had to be removed when the railway was built. By 1845, after numerous owners, the mill stood empty. The surviving building was used for fulling, but from 1883 until closure in 1939, it became a flock mill. The present building is dated 1883 just below the eave and the style and stonework is consistent throughout.

Aqueduct, Avoncliff (R), *c.* 1910. The view, taken from the lane, faces Turleigh and shows the aqueduct with the quarry tramway. The lower hillside is hidden by tall trees now, also numerous trees cover the hilltop. Much repair work has been carried out on both the bridge and the canal since this time. The aqueduct trough was not concrete lined then, nor were there any ugly railings. Retaining walls have since been built on both approaches to the aqueduct.

Cross Guns, Avoncliff (D), *c.* 1930. The Cross Guns public house claims to date from *c.* 1660. Although the deeds state that it was built in about 1612, the fireplace has been dated even further back in time. No longer an Ushers inn, it has changed little since this picture was taken. The nearest building is used as kitchens. The pitch of the roof has changed and dormer windows have been added. Also, a big chimney has replaced the flue. The view is partly obscured by trees now.

Old Court Hotel, Avoncliff, *c.* 1930. This was originally a group of weavers' houses built in 1762, but in 1836 they were converted into the Bradford Union Workhouse. During the First World War it became a convalescent home and in 1922 opened as a hotel. After closure in 1948, it returned to separate houses, having undergone much restoration. Renamed Ancliffe Square, the greenery and rose bushes have gone, so too has the portico. Alas, the stonework has been painted an unsightly buff colour.

Hospital, Avoncliff, 1917. As mentioned in the previous caption, the weavers' houses were used as a convalescent home during the First World War. This view shows some of the recuperating soldiers and their nursing staff there at that time. The men arrived at Avoncliff by train and when they were well enough they could use a Red Cross boat in order to travel to and from Bradford-on-Avon.

seven

Iford
and Westwood

Bridge and Manor, Iford (D), *c.* 1910. This view has changed little, although the greenery has now been removed from the bridge and house. Most notable is the absence of the statue of Britannia on the bridge. It was put there by Harold Peto, who also designed the manor gardens. A gardener holding a rake can be seen just to the left of the large block of stone, upon which the statue was placed. A number of boys can be seen sitting on the bridge parapet.

Manor House, Iford (D), *c.* 1930. The next three pictures were probably taken on the same day. This is the east end of the house from the gardens. The majority of the house pre-dates the Georgian frontage, which was added by Henry Chandler in around 1730. From 1543 it belonged to the Horton family, until 1623 when it was bought by the Hungerfords of Farleigh Hungerford. Parts of the house are reputed to date to the 1300s, although the two gables are of seventeenth-century origin.

Manor House, Iford (D), *c*. 1930. This one shows a much closer view of a part of the house shown in the previous picture. Sunlight shines through the slatted floor of the balcony casting a shadow on the stonework below. This is no longer possible as the slatted floor is no longer there. The loggia was another addition of the early 1900s. The statue in the foreground is no longer present.

Manor House Gardens, Iford (D), *c.*1930. Here is a view along the Great Terrace. The terrace was previously a grass walk and was created after John Gaisford bought the manor in 1777. The gazebo, which can be seen at the end, was also built at this time, but not in this location. After falling into neglect, the house and gardens were restored when Harold Peto took possession of the manor in 1903. In more recent times the gardens once again fell into decay, but have been superbly restored since.

Upper Westwood, *c.*1925. This sleepy view is of Upper Westwood and is looking towards Bradford-on-Avon. The property behind the wall on the left is Rose Cottage and next to it is the end of some further cottages. The façade seen here has since been disfigured by the addition of a large garage door. The house on the right has altered little although it originally had a front door that faced out onto the road, like the cottage behind it.

Wesleyan Chapel, Upper Westwood, *c.*1905. The old chapel is now so different I actually walked past without recognising it. Converted in 1972 to a residence named Broadview, many alterations were made. The front wall has been removed along with the porch. The front door was blocked up and the windows altered to form four smaller ones. One feature that did not deserve to be removed was the plaque of 1862. Note the old gabled house to the left, replaced in 1907 by Hope Cottage.

Greenhill House, Upper Westwood, 1951. Further on along the lane towards Bradford-on-Avon is the superb Greenhill House. Now returned to its original title of Well House, it remains just as seen here. The west wing is a recent addition to this eighteenth-century building, whilst the east wing was a seventeenth-century cottage which was increased from a single to a two storey structure in about 1910. This view is very deceptive as the lane crosses between the house and the large hedges.

Lower Westwood (Y), 1912. These are the first cottages that you pass as you enter the village from Freshford. Numerous changes have occurred here since. The rag stone kerbing has gone and the nearest doorway has been made into a window. The gabled house barely visible just beyond Rhodes Cottage (with white window surrounds) has been pulled down and the house where the girl standing on the step dressed in white has also gone. On the right the village school can be seen.

Lower Westwood (Y), 1912. The photographer has now moved a short distance along the road and is stood close to the village school. The house on the far left was the village post office for many years. The remainder of the terrace is little changed and even the railings remain unaltered. The house behind the row of children is no longer standing, whilst the old small cottage to its right has had a much larger building added to it.

Westwood School (Y), 1912. The photographer has now turned his attention to the school. The left side was the original building, which is dated 1841 and to the right is the extension of 1892. Following the building of a new school, it closed in 1976 and has become a private house. A few alterations have been made, the most prominent being the blocking-up of central sections of the large windows. Also, the sloping section of parapet above the doorway has been removed.

Westwood Manor.

Westwood Manor, *c.*1905. The manor in its earliest form consisted of two houses, which were owned by the Dean and Chapter of Winchester. They were joined together in the sixteenth-century, creating a grand house. By the 1700s the house went into decline and by 1833 it was used as a farmhouse. Restoration commenced after its purchase by Mr Lister in 1912, which included removing all the greenery seen here. Following his death in 1956, the National Trust were bequeathed the property.

Westwood Church and Manor (P), *c.*1905. This scene has changed little to this day, although some of the tombstones have been lost. Of those that remain, many are illegible. Parts of the church of St Mary the Virgin date as far back in time as the twelfth-century, although the chapel and tower were not added until the sixteenth-century. The manor can be seen in the background, with a similar growth of creeper to that in the previous picture.

Westwood Vicarage, 1905. The postcard was posted on 20 April 1905 and describes 'our new house'. It was actually built in 1878–9 by Voisey & Wills, but was designed by a Flemish architect. Now called the Old Vicarage, it was sold by the church in 1965. This is the view from the roadside corner facing towards the church. The ivy has mostly been removed and the bleak surroundings have been replaced by a beautiful garden, with a large tree growing in the foreground.

Elms Cross House (P), *c.*1913. Construction began in 1908, but in 1913, whilst still incomplete, it was gutted by fire. The structure behind the policeman was replaced by a large tower. The blaze was started in various parts of the building and blame was placed upon the suffragette movement although no one was ever held to account for the crime. It was rebuilt in 1922 and later became the Granby Hotel. In August 1947 it was gutted by fire again, and then rebuilt as a private residence.

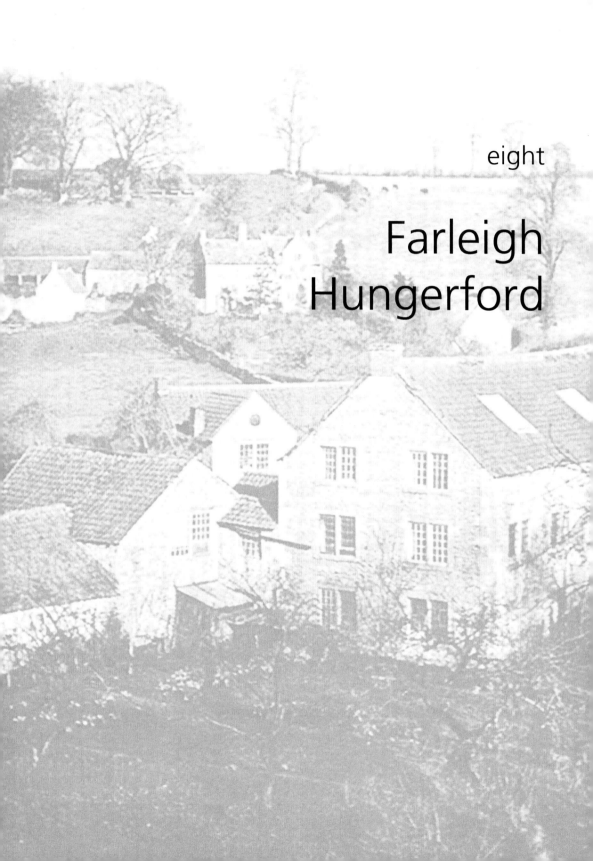

eight

Farleigh Hungerford

Distant View of the Castle (D), *c*.1930. This photograph was taken looking from the river bridge. Currently, only the gatehouse can be seen, due to the numerous trees that have grown up since. The castle's central building is the Priest's House, which was built in 1430. In the late 1600s it was extended towards the south-east tower and is currently used as a museum. The ramshackle buildings to the left of the river have long gone, to be replaced by stone cottages.

General View, *c*.1920. This scene is looking from the main road through the village. The other side of the buildings shown in the previous picture can be seen here on the right side of the lane. New stone cottages have replaced these. With the mill already demolished, the castle can readily be seen overlooking the site. Well-tended gardens now occupy the site of the cloth mills, which stood to the left of the wall.

Cloth Mill, *c.*1906. There was a fulling mill here as early as 1548. Occupied by James Noad in the 1790s, the mill burnt down on 27 April 1798 and was subsequently totally rebuilt. A steam engine had been added to the factory by 1821. By 1834 it was let to James Moore. There was a separate fulling mill further downstream just under the castle wall. To the right of the mill buildings are Riverbank Cottage, dating from 1871, the chapel of 1850 and the former post office.

Farleigh Castle Mills (P), *c.*1905. Following a second fire in 1849, Gordon Jones and Slater, then Charles Slater & Co. ran the mills. Before the fire the mill was four storeys high, but can be seen here just two storeys tall, although windows belonging to the third storey can be seen. In 1910 the owner retired after his son was accidentally killed in London whilst trying to sell cloth. Although advertised for sale in April 1910, no time was wasted in their demolition soon after.

WATERCRESS COTTAGE.

Watercress Cottage (D), *c*.1905. This lovely cottage, built in the shadow of the castle, dates back to the seventeenth-century and may have been built with stone from the castle. The wall and shed adjoining the cottage have gone, to be replaced by an extension to the property. Despite having a thatched roof, it is by no means in harmony with the original building. The covered structures on the left have also gone and the path now climbs a series of steps before passing through the garden gate.

Farleigh Castle (D), *c.*1930. Here we can see the castle in all its glory from the top of Rowley Lane. Up until 1702 the castle was intact, but by the time Joseph Houlton bought it in 1730, it had begun to fall into decay and the materials were used for other purposes. The north-east tower fell down in 1797 after being undermined by locals plundering the stone.

East Gate, Farleigh Castle, *c.*1910. The gatehouse is surely the most prominent landmark in the locality and dates back to the period *c.*1420-30, when the outer court of the castle was constructed. It has now been stripped of growth and this has resulted in the sickle badge of the Hungerford family and their coat of arms, positioned just above the window, becoming visible once again. For about two hundred years from *c.*1610-20, there was a house located to the left side of the gatehouse. This postcard was one of a series produced by the Bath Tramways Ltd.

View from the Castle (D), *c*.1930. The view seen here is not too distant from that in the previous picture. Nearest the camera is Castle House, which has been recently extended. The site where the mill stood is clearly visible to the left of the tree. In the background is the present road, with one of the two bridges located behind the tree. It was constructed in 1760 as a turnpike road. The old buildings on the left of the lane were in a poor state of repair by this time.

Farleigh Castle (P), *c*.1905. This is a closer view of the once derelict chapel. This fourteenth-century chapel was originally the parish church of St Leonard until a new one was constructed in the middle of the following century. Apart from clearance of the vegetation, little has changed. The sixteenth-century gateway to the chapel had a gable built over it in the nineteenth-century and more recently a replacement cross has been affixed to the top of this gable.

Farleigh Castle, *c.*1905. Once inside the grounds, this is a view of the most complete part of the castle. The main difference, apart from the removal of all the creeper, is that the grassy area in the foreground has been excavated to reveal many of the foundation walls and stone paving relating to the late fourteenth-century inner court. On the left is the south-east tower, whilst on the right is the heavily overgrown gatehouse, in between is the chapel.

Interior of Chapel, Farleigh Castle (P), *c.*1905. Looking into the chapel from the top of the steps, visitors today will no longer see it looking like this. The arms and armour were taken to London as their condition was found to be deteriorating. The font was brought here from the parish church in 1833, although it is thought that it resided here previously. To the right of the window is a large wall painting and the Hungerford coat of arms can be seen above the window.

Old Oak Chest, Farleigh Castle (P), *c*.1905. The Hungerford family left this impressive chest, along with the one in the previous picture, in the chapel long after they sold the estate. The style of the object would suggest it belongs to the early sixteenth-century. Many of the items in the chapel once belonged to the Hungerford family or were collected from the locality to be display here. As with the armour shown previously, the chest is no longer kept here.

The Sleeping Earls, Farleigh Castle (P), *c*.1905. This somewhat gruesome postcard shows the vault beneath the chapel, containing members of the Hungerford family. The wooden outer coffins have long since perished, leaving only the lead inner coffins, four of which have faces moulded onto them. The infants were originally placed on top of their mothers' coffins. Of all the coffins, only Lady Jane Hungerford, who died in 1664, can positively be identified as lying here.

Post Office (D), *c*.1920. The sign for the post office is clearly visible just above the two cross-shaped tombstones. Long since closed, it is now called Church View. To its left is Church Cottage, whilst to the right is White Horse View. Behind the gate is the Old Coach House. The tree is no longer with us, nor is the village school, which is on the far right. Sadly, all these buildings have now lost their stone roof tiles.

Farleigh Hungerford House (P) *c*.1905. This vast house dates back well into the seventeenth-century, but now has a more modern frontage, which replaced gabled fronts on the east and south sides. The Hungerford family owned the house until 1686, yet it was not until 1716 that the Houlton family resided here. Lt-Col. John Houlton enlarged and altered the house in the early nineteenth-century and it remains very much the same today, apart from the removal of the ivy.

The Hungerford Arms, *c.*1930. Dating from the mid-1700s, this public house previously occupied only the most distant building, but in around 1900 the other two cottages were acquired so as to expand the premises. Little has changed since, although the nearest doorway has been blocked up and an extra window added to the far right cottage. Also, a car park has replaced the metal-roofed shed. Sadly, with the recent closure of the brewery, it is no longer an Ushers inn.

Farleigh Service Station 1925. This petrol filling station opened on the A36 Warminster Road in 1925 and was run by Messrs Perry and Bendall. From 1927 until the present day, the Ball family has owned it. Located at the junction with the Trunk Road and a lane leading to Farleigh Hungerford, the premises were rebuilt in 1960 and again in 1992, so it has now become a thoroughly modern filling station, selling Esso fuels.